CW00542768

PRAYERS OF ELVIS

Madeleine Wilson

Shalom Publishing

Published by Shalom Publishing

First published August 2002

Any enquiries about this book, please contact:
Madeleine Wilson
"Shalom"
10 Primrose Lane
Wolverhampton
WV10 8RS
England, UK

Email: prayers@elvis.com
www.elvisgospel.com

ISBN 0-9543230-0-9

Printed in the UK by: The Birches Printers Limited

First reprint 2002

Contents

Dedication

To all Elvis fans worldwide, with special thanks to those who prayed
for Elvis through his most trying times.

Introduction

How this book came to be written could itself be the subject of a book. As a teenager in the 1950s, I listened to and enjoyed the music of Elvis Presley, perhaps even watching a film or two. At the time of the death of Elvis, I was a wife and mother of two young children very much involved with family matters and do not remember hearing about his death, let alone remembering where I was at the time, although I do remember the street party we had for the Queen's Silver Jubilee in 1977. I became a Christian in 1987 and was aware of the power of prayer. I had prayed for my family to be saved and by 1991 my husband and three children were all committed Christians. It wasn't until 1995 that I became aware of the importance of Elvis Presley. I had been praying for a hobby. Perhaps a somewhat strange prayer, but I felt that I needed something that I could do which would be a separate interest from my family responsibilities and help provide me with some relaxation. So it was in January 1995, whilst watching some of the programmes, which had been on TV for the Elvis 60th Birthday celebration, that it happened! I became an Elvis fan. I wept for a week after seeing the programmes. It was such a strong experience, that I prayed and asked the Lord what it was all about and felt led to start researching into Elvis' life. I discovered that not only was he brought up as a Christian, but that he was called to be an evangelist.

During my research I have been privileged to meet members of Elvis' family and friends who understood his spiritual yearnings. I have begun to understand this simple, yet complex man whom I never met, but hope to one day. I have begun to understand his calling; something, which I believe, will be a continuing, story. It is a story of dreams, hopes, passion, disappointment and ultimate victory. In this book I have tried to outline Elvis' gospel roots and his spiritual journey in the light of some of the prayers that he was known to have prayed and proposed some of the prayers he may have prayed. Within the word prayer I have included psalms and songs and other Biblical passages, as prayer is communication with God and we can do that in many ways. Where I have quoted from the Bible, I have done so from the New International Version unless otherwise stated. KJV is the King James Version and ASV is the American Standard Version.

Acknowledgements

My grateful thanks go to the following who have contributed to the writing of this book, either through personal contact and/or their own writings. Please accept my apologies if you know that you have been involved and your name does not appear. Be assured that although I may not have remembered, the Lord has!

Rex and Caroline Dyson, Marion and Joanne Carson, Dixie Locke Emmons, Becky Martin, Annie Presley, Frank and Corene Smith, Donna Presley Early, Terry Blackwood, Joe Moscheo, Sherman Andrus, Gordon Stoker, Jim Murray, Ed Enoch, Donnie Sumner, Shaun Neilson, Glen Hardin, Larry Geller, June Juanico, Rick Stanley, Peter Guralnik, Bill Burk, Ernst Jorgensen, Elaine Dundy, Bill and Gloria Gaither, Mosie Lister, Hovie Lister, Kathy Westmoreland, Stephen King, Hugh Brogan, Kenneth Osbeck, Debbie White, Jim Reid, Jerry Osborne, Billy Nashad, Anne E Nixon, Richard Harvey, Christine Darg, Tony Stone, Peter Kay, Sheila Lowe and staff at Elvis Presley Enterprises.

I am also extremely grateful for the loving support of my family, especially my husband Peter and for all our faithful prayer partners. Finally, I wish to express my undying gratitude to my Lord, Jesus Christ, without whom none of this would have been possible.

Chapter 1
Tupelo Honey – Sweet Beginnings

"He nourished them with honey from the rock" (Deuteronomy 32:13)

Many people have described Elvis as "sweet". What was the source of this "sweetness"? Perhaps it was the Holy Spirit, that "Sweet, Sweet Spirit" whom he so loved to sing about. As we shall discover, Elvis' roots were indeed sweet, though tinged with hardship.

Elvis Presley was born in a two room wooden cabin in Tupelo, Mississippi on January 8th 1935; minutes after his twin bother Jessie, who was stillborn. Elvis remained the only child of Vernon Elvis and Gladys Love Presley.

He was named Elvis after his father and Aaron in honour of Aaron Kennedy, the song leader at church, a friend of the family whom Vernon most admired. It was Aaron Kennedy who later on would encourage Elvis to learn to read well, so that he could appreciate his Bible.

Right from the beginning of his life Elvis knew that he was loved, that he was special and that one day he would do great things. During her labour pains, Gladys is reported as saying "I know it will be a boy – a boy who will be a joy to the world, I will live so my boy can live. He has a wonderful life ahead of him." Later Elvis would ask his mother, "Why was Jesse born dead and not me?" She replied, "Honey, God has plans for all of us. He took your little brother back home to heaven. One day we'll all be in home in heaven. Never forget that."

The Bible says that the tongue is an instrument of life or death and that we can choose how to use it. Elvis' parents and family always spoke well of him and in a sense prophesied his success. Mrs. Grimes, one of

his schoolteachers in Tupelo said that he was just a sweet child and that people who knew him well just loved him. She never heard anyone say anything bad about him.

The Presleys were part of an extended family and had many relatives in the area who helped each other through the years of economic depression of the 1930's.

They were descended from David Presley, who arrived in North Carolina in 1845 from Ireland. His family were originally from Scotland, but had moved to Ireland and then because of hardship caused by the potato blight, sailed to USA to seek a new and hopefully, more prosperous life.

Church going was an integral part of the Presleys' lives in the 1930s, as was the teaching of the Gospel in schools. No wonder that this part of America was known as the Bible Belt.

The 1828 edition of Webster's American Dictionary of the English Language defines the Bible as "The Book by way of eminence; the sacred volume, in which are contained the revelations of God, the principles of Christian faith and the rules of practise. It consists of two parts, called the Old and New testaments. The Bible should be the standard of language as well of faith."

Elvis was brought up to believe that "The fear of the Lord is pure. The ordinances of the Lord are sure and altogether righteous. They are more precious than gold, than much pure gold, they are sweeter than honey, than honey from the comb. By them is your servant

"What's wrong with Christianity today? We're still of this world, not separated from it as we should be. Separate yourself from the world. We've got to separate ourselves from the world before we have revival in our hearts. Get to where nothing matters but God."

Although Elvis could not have heard this particular sermon, he would be aware of its advice and later in the difficult times, would remove himself from the world and retreat to the sanctuary of his beloved home Graceland in Memphis.

Until the Assemblies of God Church built its baptistry people were baptised in the local town creek. When they had built the baptistry, the fire truck would come to fill it for them.

Several sources mention that Elvis was baptised in 1944; some say, baptised in the Holy Spirit. Frank Smith is adamant that he did not baptise Elvis. Dixie Locke, Elvis' girlfriend whom he met at the First Assemblies of God Church in Memphis in 1954 recalls that baptism in the Holy Spirit and speaking in tongues was taught at church and they were exposed to its manifestation in others and just expected that it would happen one day. As far as she knew Elvis was not baptised in water whilst at their church and neither of them spoke in tongues. Dixie was not baptised in the Holy Spirit herself until she was twenty-six years old.

Baptism in the Holy Spirit is not something we choose to do on a certain time and date like water baptism, which is undertaken by believers in response to Jesus' command to repent and be baptised, but rather it is an experience direct from God, one of the manifestations of which is speaking in tongues.

In 1946, the Presleys moved from East Tupelo to Mulberry Alley, near to Shake Rag (a very poor part of Tupelo where the coloured people lived). There the 11-year-old would slip out of his mom's sight and go over to Shake Rag with friends and listen to a different kind of music, which expressed the pain and hurt of generations, but which still had a strong vein of hope. Elvis would have noticed that the singing in the churches of the blacks was somehow more exuberant and expressive than the music he heard in his own church. A few months later they moved to North Green Street to a "whites only" designated area in a "respectable" coloured neighbourhood.

Peter Guralnick, in "Last Train to Memphis", says of the regular church revivals held in North Green Street, "People would come from all over, dressed up in their finest regalia, the women in pink and yellow and hot fuchsia, wearing fantastic feathered boa hats and carrying their weight without apology, the preachers preaching without anything to hold them back. Getting lost in their Bible, chanting, breathing, snorting rhythmically, gutturally, breathlessly, until their voices soared off into song. You didn't have to go inside to get the feeling, the sound, the sense, the allure were all around you. You only had to walk up the street and the street was rocking. There was really nothing like it, you had to hand it to the coloured people, they really knew how to live. If you lived on North Green Street, you breathed it in as natural as air – after a while you got used to it, it became yours too, it *was almost like being in church*."

Perhaps that is why later when they moved to Memphis, Elvis would still like to visit the black churches to hear the lively, powerful singing and ecstatic preaching.

Singing wasn't just for church. The family would often sing at home and around 1946 Elvis and his family would attend Saturday afternoon Jamborees in downtown Tupelo. These were organised by the local radio station WELO and were a kind of amateur talent hour that was broadcast from the courthouse. There were also the popular Gospel Quartet singings to be enjoyed.

Elvis was soon to venture into other expressions of music. For his 11th birthday Elvis' parents bought him a guitar. Several people were involved with teaching Elvis to play the instrument, including Frank Smith, "Mississippi Slim", a local singer and comedian who Elvis admired and with whose brother James Ausborn, Elvis went to school. Elvis' uncles, Johnny and Vester, also tutored him. It was also around this time that Elvis started to play the piano. The family of course would not have been able to afford one at home, but he had plenty of opportunity at school and church to learn to play. He was self-taught. Once when asked who taught Elvis to play the piano Glen Hardin, one of Elvis' pianists in the '70s, said "no-one, he was a terrible piano player!" Of course by Glen's professional standard he was, but Elvis preferred the piano to the guitar and played well enough to enjoy himself and even occasionally accompanied himself on the piano in concerts.

The discipline imposed by his parents was rigorous by today's standards, but it worked. One admonishment that Elvis remembered was the first time he stole something. He took two empty cola bottles from a neighbour's porch. His mother questioned him about the bottles and he admitted his wrongdoing. Gladys took him by the hand to return the bottles. That was embarrassment enough, but

his mother then informed him that he was to confess his sin to the church next Sunday morning. The fateful morning arrived and a tearful Elvis whispered his wrongdoing to the entire Assemblies of God congregation and ran out of the church. He never again took anything without permission.

At an early age he learned to pray, both in church and at home. He would have heard his parents praying. Vernon, in an interview with Good Housekeeping said "He (Elvis) had developed acute tonsillitis with such a high fever; he was on the verge of convulsions. Gladys and I were afraid that we were going to lose him." Even the doctor had given up on him and suggested they call in another. They did not do that, but instead "My wife and I turned in prayer to the greatest healer of all, God. I do believe in miracles so that day I prayed to God that he would miraculously heal our child. My wife and I prayed together and separately, and by night I could see that Elvis was better"

Elvis' Aunt Nash, Vernon's sister who was nine years old when Elvis was born and spent many hours with the family, said "Prayer has always been an important part of life for the Presley family. I can remember Vernon on his knees in church praying. I heard him so many times in his bedroom praying. When Elvis was small Elvis would lay his hands on Vernon and Gladys when they were sick and pray for them. He would tell them 'Jesus will make it all better'."

Elvis was a dreamer. Sitting on the porch with his Aunt Nash, they would talk about what they would like to do when they grew up. Elvis said he wanted to be a truck driver and a singer and Nash said she would like to be a nurse and a gospel singer, Nash says… "one of those people became a pretty popular singer and it wasn't me!" Aunt Nash did fulfil her dream, though in a slightly different way. She became a gospel preacher and was ordained as a minister in the Assemblies of God in 1974 and pastored a church in Walls, Mississippi. Elvis also said that he was going to buy his mom and dad a big house and many cars, and as we all know that came true and more. The Bible says that the Lord can do more than we can ever imagine or dream of.

The role which the church played in the lives of the Presleys, can be exemplified by the following recollections of Annie Presley, a close relative and friend of Gladys. We visited her in her home in Tupelo and she told us, "At church each child was given a pocket New Testament, then later a full Bible, which they would bring to church. Apart from the Sunday services we had prayer meetings and Bible studies during the week. The church members would vote on such matters as the purchase of a piano. The dress and behaviour code was very strict. People were turned out of the church for immorality." She told us that a gospel group, the Sunflower Sisters from Memphis visited their church and were disapproved of for their permed hair and "fancy" dress.

The people believed in healing prayer, which was a regular occurrence. Annie's husband, Sales, became very ill and the church prayed for him, but there seemed to be no improvement. Finally one of the Elders of the church decided to fast and pray for five days and nights and said God told him that it was Sales' time to die. Although in one way it was not good news, it was a great relief to know that Sales would soon be out of pain. Sales died at the age of 33. Annie was in hospital with him. His final prayer was "God, I can't stand the pain. I surrender my life to you. Please take care of my wife and children." He went unconscious and died a few hours later.

Annie then went on to tell of the goodness of God in looking after her and her children. One day, the eve of Thanksgiving, Annie made some biscuits and gravy, using up the last food they had in the house. She told her children to eat everything up as they had no more food and they must now trust in God for their next meals. They went to bed and slept late. Meanwhile, at the Thanksgiving service the next day, the Pastor asked the congregation to pray and ask God to lay on their hearts anyone who was in need that day. One of Annie's relatives, whom they had not seen for some time thought of them and took round some food. One of the children, much to Annie's embarrassment, looked through the food parcel and said "Mom, if there was some shortening, we could make some biscuits." The relative then realised that there was no food in the house and came back with more groceries. Families would always help each other out with meals if they knew of the need, and sometimes it was God himself who gave them that information directly.

Nine years after Sales' death, Annie married another Presley, Sales' cousin, and had a daughter by him. According to Annie, the Presleys were attending the Second Baptist Church when they left Tupelo in 1948. Annie visited Gladys several times in Memphis after Elvis had started earning a lot of money and had bought Graceland for himself and his parents. Gladys confided in Annie that she would give anything to have to trust in God again for their physical needs. "Money don't mean anything," Gladys observed. All she could do now, was to sit and look out of the window.

We had a good time with Annie and noticed that on her front door was a plaque saying, "Welcome to the Presleys" and "As for me and my house, we will serve the Lord". Annie's grief over her husband's illness and death had not turned her against God, but she felt some dissatisfaction with the Assemblies of God Church, which she eventually left in favour of a Baptist church.

Although they suffered economic hardship, Elvis' childhood in Tupelo was indeed sweet and full of life. Elvis displayed a sweetness and innocence about which Elaine Dundy says, "that remarkable indestructible, almost *inhuman* innocence that self perpetuating that self regenerating would remain with him all his life". One could say that it is indeed not human, because it is divine; it is the sweetness of the Holy Spirit.

In November 1948 Vernon, Gladys and Elvis, along with other family members, moved to Memphis. They started attending the Church of the Lord Jesus Christ on 7th Street, pastored by Rev. Rex Dyson. Having met Reverend Dyson, I am convinced that his passionate preaching had a great effect on the young teenage Elvis. Elvis' Sunday school teacher was Marion Carson who remembers Elvis as a quiet, well-behaved young man. Marion was also a good friend of Vernon's and being a painter and decorator, he would often see him at the United Paint Company in north Memphis where Vernon worked loading cans.

Rex Dyson remembers Vernon and Gladys more than he does Elvis, though he does recall the time Elvis came up to be baptised.

When I asked him how the Presleys came to be at his church he said "Gladys and Vernon got acquainted with me when they would come and listen to me preach every Sunday afternoon in Court Square on Main Street, all summer long. They drove up from Tupelo every weekend." (Perhaps this explains the reports that the Presleys did not attend church so much just before they left Tupelo to live in Memphis. Perhaps they drove up every weekend to do some scouting for jobs and accommodation and also to look for a good church).

I also wondered how the Presleys would know of Rex when they were in Tupelo and he was preaching in Memphis. I later learned that even in those days Rex was a very well known and respected preacher and people would travel miles to hear him. I also understand that the evangelist Rex Humbard was named after him.

Rex Dyson had bought the First Pentecostal Church on 4th and Keele in 1936 and then in 1949, built the Church of Jesus Christ on 7th Street. He could not remember whether or not the Presleys attended the church on 4th and Keele, but he definitely remembers that they attended the 7th Street church for that was where he baptised Vernon, Gladys and Elvis around 1950. He says, "I baptised Vernon and Gladys first. I had them in the baptistry. Elvis came up to the baptistry and he said, "I want to be baptised". I baptised all three of them. Rex's wife, Caroline interjects, "All three were together in the baptistry – it was quite full!"

I asked how Elvis' parents came to be baptised. Rex said, "I preached them in. They didn't know anything about baptism in Jesus' name. I preached them under conviction and they came and was baptised."

In 1950 the Dysons lived in Woodlawn Street, just opposite Humes High where Elvis and two of their boys attended. Caroline says that Elvis and her sons and one or two other boys from the church including a boy named Sonny Prater went to school together. She says, "Sonny told me many a time, he said, 'we all just shared our lunch money and shared our lunches or whatever we had.' So he (Elvis) come up poorly. He wasn't born with a silver spoon in his mouth."

Rex recalls, "During those years Elvis got him a little band, a string band, and my boy here (showing a photo of his son, David) played the steel guitar in Elvis' little string band." Caroline continues, "They finally ended up in the Goodwin Institute, the place where they had musical things going on. I remember it very well because my mother passed away in 1955 and dad here had to go to the Goodwin Institute to get our son David who was down there with Elvis playin'."

When asked if Elvis ever discussed with them about what he wanted to do with his life, Caroline says, "He talked to my sons. If he did discuss that they never told us. You know how boys are. It's all kind of hush hush. They don't want anyone to know what they're talking about!"

The Dysons kept track of Elvis until he went in the army and then had no more contact, although they tried several times.

Rex speculates, "Elvis could have been a wonderful... he could have done just as much for God as he did for the world out there if he had just lived right and done right. There's no doubt (that he was called to be a preacher)."

"I can say for sure, his mother was a real Holy Ghost Christian. I don't know if Vernon ever received the baptism of the Holy Ghost or not and I don't know if Elvis did or not, he didn't whilst he was at this church. That's between them and the Lord. We are not to judge. Elvis could have done a great work for God if he would have just really lived for God, that's the whole tragedy".

Caroline adds "I always did believe that Elvis was God-minded, if you know what I mean. The young people back then, they didn't talk about shooting and banging up things. They talked about church and preachers and such like. They all played (church) music. They would get together in that trailer in our back yard and oh, all the noise with their singin'! They would really go at it! The boys that they'd hang out with were like two of mine, all naturally preachers. I imagine that in Elvis' mind the same thoughts were. My (five) boys all turned out to be preachers. It should have been the same with Elvis."

Chapter 2
The Slippery Slope – Memphis Meanderings

"Only be careful and watch yourselves closely, so that you do not forget the things your eyes have seen or let them slip from your heart as long as you live" (Deuteronomy 4:9)

The move to Memphis was a good one for the Presleys. There were plenty of job opportunities so they were able to sustain a reasonable income and they had a welcoming church to belong to where they were encouraged by the powerful preaching of Reverend Rex Dyson. In 1953, however, Rex believed that the Lord had called him Israel to set up a mission in Bethlehem. Rex says that Vernon begged him not to go, partly most probably fearing for Rex's safety, but also not wanting to lose such a wonderful pastor. Rex was convinced of his call to Israel and went for several months. When he returned, the Presleys were no longer attending the church.

As Caroline Dyson says, Elvis was God-minded. He was particularly interested in the Old Testament of the Bible and the role of the Jews in God's plans. It was no surprise then that he made immediate friends with the Fruchters, when in the Spring of 1953 the Presleys moved into a ground floor apartment below the Fruchters. Alfred Fruchter was founder of the Orthodox Memphis Hebrew Academy and according to Larry Geller, one of Elvis' friends; Elvis' Pentecostal roots showed as he asked the Rabbi, "You don't believe in Jesus, do you?" To which the Rabbi replied, "I believe he was a great man – one of the greatest of the Jewish prophets". A puzzled Elvis then asked, "So why don't you accept him? If he was a Rabbi and you're a Rabbi, shouldn't you stick together?" The rest of Elvis family also came to know and love the Fruchters and sometimes would sit down with them for their Shabbat meal. I should imagine Elvis had some questions about prayer for this friendly Rabbi.

As well as attending church, the Presleys enjoyed attending the monthly all-night gospel singings at the Ellis Auditorium and that is where Elvis came to love the singing of the Blackwood Brothers and the Statesmen, especially JD Sumner and Jake Hess. He particularly liked the flamboyant stage presentation of some of the singers.

In January 1954 Elvis started to attend the First Assemblies of God Church on McLemore, most probably because it was the church which the Blackwood Brothers attended, and although it was two miles from his home, the church organised rides for those without their own transport. It was there that he met Dixie Locke who became his girl friend. Elvis regularly attended both the Sunday school and the worship service. Elvis and Dixie were in different classes, as Dixie was four years younger than Elvis, but they 'noticed' each other and soon started dating. When I met Dixie, she not only still attended the church but was also the Church Secretary. She very graciously shared some of her memories of Elvis with us. She said that most of the dates she went on with Elvis were church related and that they talked a lot about their Christian faith. Elvis had no problems with the Gospel and he truly believed that Jesus was the only Son of God and that He died for our sins, so that we may have everlasting life. They both attended the Ellis gospel singings and even an Oral Roberts Crusade in May 1954. It was to Dixie at his mother's funeral in August 1958, that Elvis blurted out that he would like to walk away from it all, but that "there are too many people that depend on me, I'm too far in to get out".

In July 1954, Elvis recorded "That's All Right Mama" at Sun Studios. It immediately became a local hit, and very soon Elvis was recording more songs which people just loved to listen to and he started travelling around the south doing one night shows. In March 1956 he had his first number 1 hit with "Heartbreak Hotel" and by May 1956 he was rich enough to be able to buy his family a house (in Audubon Drive), thus fulfilling one of his dreams. In those two short years he had shot to stardom, but had become more removed from his spiritual roots. He could no longer attend church as he was travelling most Sundays and even if he tried to the fans would cause too much commotion, which Elvis felt was disrespectful to God. With this hectic life style, even his prayer life and Bible reading suffered. June Juanico, his girlfriend in 1956, told me that she never saw Elvis read a religious book and they didn't pray together.

Elvis hadn't forgotten his gospel roots though. He still loved gospel music and asked that the Jordanaires gospel singers to be his backing group, to which they agreed. When he was asked to take part in the Ed Sullivan show in New York in 1957 the producers did not want any gospel songs. What would it do for Elvis' image being so far removed from the raw energy of "Hound Dog" and "Heartbreak Hotel"? Elvis insisted however that he sang "Peace in the Valley" (apparently he had promised his mother that he would sing it for her). This led to the production of the top selling "Peace In the Valley" EP, from which we can deduce that going for the gospel does not only not harm one, but is of benefit. It is interesting to note that Elvis was awarded only three Grammys for his recordings and that they were all for his gospel music.

Apart from his name and his title the "King of Rock and Roll", perhaps the next most well known fact about Elvis is his home of 20 years, his beloved Graceland. Graceland was designed and built in 1939 by Dr. and Mrs. Moore in the Whitehaven District of Memphis. It was named after Grace Toof, Mrs. Moore's aunt. The house was designed and planned with music in mind for their daughter Ruth Marie, who played the piano and harp and who eventually joined the Memphis Symphony Orchestra. The living rooms were built large enough to hold musical soirees. The Moores moved out in 1957 and when Elvis went to see the property, it was being used for meetings by Graceland Christian Church. When Elvis moved in to Graceland later in 1957, the Church built another property next door, on land given to them by Mrs. Moore. Later, the church moved to another part of Memphis and the building now houses the headquarters of Elvis Presley Enterprises Inc. It seems that Elvis could not escape his Christian roots; even his new home was a church! It was certainly a haven of rest for Elvis, though most often a hive of activity as Elvis had, by his own choice, his extended family including his parents, grandmother and aunt and some friends living there.

By now Elvis was feeling the slippery slope. On Easter Sunday 1957, Elvis sought out Pastor James Hamill, his pastor at the First Assemblies of God Church, and said, "Pastor, I am the most miserable young man you have ever seen. I have got more money than I can ever spend. I have thousands of fans out there, and I have a lot of people who call themselves my friends, but I am miserable. I am not doing a lot of things you taught me and I am

Madeleine Wilson with Annie Presley at Annie's home in Tupelo.

The scripture on this plaque which is on the front door of Annie's home is from Joshua 24:15.

Elvis in his Sunday best, age around twelve, with girlfriend Magdalene Morgan.
The photo was taken in Tupelo by Corene Smith, the wife of Reverend Frank Smith, whose
church the Presleys attended.

Left to right: Caroline Dyson, Peter Wilson, Reverend Rex Dyson. Rex Dyson is the Minister who baptised Vernon, Gladys and Elvis. This photo taken in 2000, shows Rex in his 101st year.

Left to right: Madeleine Wilson, Joanne Carson, Marion Carson, in the Carson's home in Memphis. Marion was Elvis' Sunday School teacher in 7th Street Church.

Elvis' Mother's grave in Forest Hills Cemetery, Memphis. Note that the footstone is carved with a Christian cross and a Star of David. *Photo by kind permission of Jim Reid.*

doing some things you taught me not to do". This could be seen as a public prayer of confession, but there is an even more public prayer, which we shall see later.

Meanwhile Elvis had started to make films in Hollywood and by the end of 1957 had given up touring. One reason for this was that he was called up into the Army in March 1958. While stationed in Texas, he did attend church with his friend Eddie Fadal, but then arguably the greatest tragedy of his life occurred. His beloved mother who had not been well for sometime and was just as miserable about her son's lifestyle as he was, died. Her funeral, as was Elvis' was held in Graceland and he asked the Blackwoods to be present to sing, which they did including many more songs than originally planned. Elvis was for quite some time inconsolable, but his public prayer, in the form of the inscription, which he had carved later on the footstone of his mother's grave, showed that he had come to accept the death of his mother. The inscription says "NOT MINE BUT THY WILL BE DONE". Elvis would have been very familiar with this scripture, as it is what Jesus prays in the garden of Gethsemane, the night before his crucifixion. Jesus knew what was going to happen to him and was struggling with the contemplation of the pain, both physical and spiritual, which he would endure. He, like us, was human and had a free will, but He chose to submit to God's will, (for Him to be crucified, thus setting all men free from the bondage of sin). Perhaps Elvis identified with this situation of choosing to agree with God. Although he could not understand why the Lord should take his mother at such a young age (she was only in her early forties), he publicly acknowledged that he accepted God's way. Incidentally the footstone also has a Christian cross and a Star of David engraved on it.

Just a month after Gladys died, Elvis went to Germany. He lived off base with his father and grandmother, Minnie Mae, so would have the continuing wisdom and strength of that strong Christian lady to help him. I can find no record of him attending church whilst he was in Germany, though I assume that the base had a chapel. The death of his mother, leading to the dearth of such close Christian fellowship in his life, would certainly have made that slope much more slippery.

Apparently it was also in Germany that Elvis was introduced to prescription drugs, "uppers", to keep awake during the bitter winter watches at the Russian front. On his return to the USA in March 1960, Elvis' fears of having been forgotten by his fans soon evaporated as he was given a rapturous welcome.

It seems that most of the sixties, making what many describe as rubbish movies, (though I love them, they are good family entertainment – a rare commodity these days) was just as difficult spiritually and emotionally for Elvis as were the later fifties. Despite his own difficulties Elvis prayed for many people during these years, he prayed for healing and people were healed, he counselled and prayed for people who were having marriage difficulties or who were depressed and feeling lonely. He would tell them of God's great love for them and how they could enjoy life if they just trusted the Lord. He had the Meditation Garden built at Graceland in 1965; a peaceful place (even today with hundreds of fans milling around). His entourage, known as "The Memphis Mafia", although not on the whole partaking in Elvis' love of the Gospel, certainly recognised his zeal and enthusiasm and bought him a statue of Jesus for the Meditation Garden.

His relentless search for "the Truth", led him into studying other philosophies and religions, which only served to confuse him even more. There were a few highlights, however. He was able to have a few gospel songs included in the movies and he recorded two gospel albums, "His Hand in Mine" in 1960 and "How Great Though Art" in 1966.

The later sixties proved to be more encouraging. On May 1st 1967 he married his sweetheart, Priscilla Beaulieu whom he had met in Germany. Exactly nine months later their beautiful daughter Lisa Marie was born. Elvis was ecstatic and somewhat overawed by this little bundle of joy. In the summer of 1968, he started recording for a Christmas TV show, produced by Steve Binder, who could see the potential in Elvis for doing more than just singing a few Christmas carols. To accommodate Elvis' love of gospel music there was a whole section devoted to gospel songs. These were; "Sometimes I Feel Like a Motherless Child", "Where Could I Go But To The Lord", "Up Above My Head (There's Music In The Air)" and "Saved", all of which Elvis would be able to identify with and the latter in which he pronounces several times, with great gusto, "I'm Saved!" In the same show, however, he also sang, "I'm evil", from the song "Trouble". Perhaps a reflection of the spiritual confusion which was inside?

The finale of the programme is the beautiful song "If I Can Dream" written at the last minute, for Elvis by W Earl Brown. Elvis sings with such vigour about the yearning for a better land where brothers walk hand in hand, where doubt and fear are blown away. This song is describing heaven! Yet the song parts company with the gospel as it proclaims that, "as long as a man has the strength to dream, then he can redeem his soul and fly". Elvis would know that man cannot be redeemed through his own efforts, and yet he sings this with such passion, one thinks he might actually burst. Perhaps again this is an insight into how far Elvis had strayed from his strong belief in the redeeming power of the cross.

This show originally slated as "Singer presents Elvis" was universally accepted as "The '68 Comeback Special". It did indeed seem that Elvis had come back from the mire of those films he so hated and was back in front of his fans again, with whom he had such a great rapport.

Elvis continued to pray for and counsel his family, friends and even fans, though after the initial triumph of the three years or so back on tour, it became clear that it was Elvis himself who was very much in need of prayer. By January 1973, for the "Aloha from Hawaii" satellite TV broadcast to the world, this was evident and I know that many people from all over the world prayed for his salvation and to help him through those difficult times.

Elvis did pray for himself too, especially just before he went on stage. He prayed that he would please his audience. On one occasion before a concert when he was to sing "How Great Thou Art", but was concerned at not being able to hit the high notes. Kathy Westmoreland one of his backup singers, suggested they kneel down and ask the Lord to help him. When the time came for the song, Elvis hit the notes perfectly and he turned round to Kathy and gave her a wink. An instant answer to prayer is always gratifying!

Chapter 3
Songs of Love

"Without a song, the day would never end, without a song the road would never bend, without a song, a man ain't got a friend, without a song".   Vincent Youmans – Billy Rose – E. Eliscu

"Without a Song" was recorded by Mario Lanza on September 2nd 1951 in Hollywood. It is almost certain that Elvis knew the song as he quoted from it when he gave his acceptance speech for being voted as one of the nationís Ten Outstanding Young Men of the Year by the Jaycees, in January 1971. Elvis understood the importance of music, especially songs which have the ability to console and encourage in times of need and also to express joy and fun and celebration. Even a cursory survey of songs reveals that most songs are about love. So it can be said that most songs, not just the Gospel songs, are about God, for the Bible says that God is love. All of us are searching for that perfect love, which we believe is attainable, or otherwise why would we search?

Some songs bemoan "tainted love"; the lover who betrays us or the parents who were less than ideal. Many songs express the desire for this ideal love and some songs, the Gospel songs, do address the subject of perfect love. Most probably the best known Bible verse is John 3:16 "For God so *loved* the world that He gave His one and only Son, that who ever believes in Him shall not perish but have eternal life." That verse is the essence of the Gospel of Jesus Christ. The good news is that God loves us with a perfect love. It is certain that Elvis would have known and believed those words. They are very powerful words that strike a chord in many hearts, but what does it mean? In this chapter, I hope, by referring to a few of the eighty plus gospel songs that Elvis sang, often, I believe as a prayer, to shed light on this Gospel about which Elvis was so passionate.

How Great Thou Art
(Stuart Hine)

This hymn is a wonderful proclamation of the awesomeness of God.   There are many scriptures, which deal with this, but here is one of the most succinct:

"Great is the Lord and most worthy of praise; his greatness no-one can fathom." *(Psalm 145:3).*

The original text of this great hymn was a poem entitled 'O Store Gud' ('Oh Mighty God'), written in 1886, by Swedish pastor, the Reverend Carl Boberg. It is believed that his inspiration for the text came from a visit to a beautiful country estate on the South coast of Sweden. He was suddenly caught in a midday thunderstorm with awe-inspiring moments of flashing violence, followed by a clear brilliant sun. Soon afterwards he heard the calm sweet songs of the birds in the nearby trees. This experience prompted the pastor to fall to his knees in humble adoration of his mighty God. He then returned home and penned the poem.

From studying the videos of Elvis singing this song, it is clear that he also felt the same adoration of this awesome God. Elvis is not just singing, he is worshipping. During a June 1977 concert, a few weeks before he died, he actually personalised the song by singing "my God how great I think you are".

The original poem was sung to an old Swedish melody, translated into several languages, and eventually, in 1948, the English version, which we know now, was created. Reverend Stuart K Hine, a native of London, England translated it from Russian, changing 'Oh

Mighty God' to 'How Great Thou Art'.

Although Elvis at one time claimed to 'know practically every religious song that's ever been written', surprisingly enough he did not know this popular hymn until one of the Jordanaires, who could see that it would suit Elvis' voice, introduced it to him and suggested that he sing it. Elvis won two Grammys with this song, one for the live version and one for the recorded album.

The natural melody and harmonies of the chorus strongly resemble some of the musical phrases in the popular gospel hymn 'Pass me not O Gentle Saviour', and are reminiscent of the Hawaiian national song 'Aloha Oe'. Elvis loved being in Hawaii and one wonders if his love for the song was also influenced by the melody.

He Touched Me
(William J. Gaither)

The title of this song was used for the wonderful two-volume video "He Touched Me – The Gospel Songs of Elvis Presley" produced by Bill Gaither and nominated for a Dove Award.

Bill Gaither wrote the song during his time as Minister of Music at South Meridian Church in Anderson, Tennessee. One Saturday night, driving home with some friends after a revival service in Huntington, Indiana, they started to discuss the meeting. Apparently, the spirit of the meeting had been unusually warm and sweet, and people had been visibly touched and changed by the Holy Spirit. One of the friends, Dr. Dale, said "Bill, there's something about the word *touch*. To think that the awesome God could touch our lives is a wonderful thing. You should write a song that says, 'He touched me; oh, He touched me'."

All that night a melody kept going through Bill's head and next morning before going to church he played the melody on the piano and sang, "He touched me; oh, He touched me, and oh the joy that fills my soul… ". He had scribbled down the lyrics to two verses and a chorus and showed them to his wife, Gloria. She suggested that he changed the line "Now I am no longer the same" to something stronger and more specific. Although Bill acknowledged her suggestion, he kept the song exactly as it had originally come to him.

The song was first recorded by Doug Oldham, and has been recorded by more artists than any other song the Gaithers have written. The artists include the Imperials. George Beverly Shea, Kate Smith, Jimmy Durante and of course Elvis Presley. It was Elvis' recording that catapulted Bill to the top of the music industry. It gave him his first Grammy nomination and a Dove award for songwriter of the year. It was said that "He Touched Me" had more impact on the listening public in 1969 than any other song recorded.

One of the reasons, I believe, for the impact of the song is that it so simply expresses the power of that wonderful moment every born again Christian experiences. That moment when the Almighty God "touches" us and our souls are filled with the joy of wonderful conviction that God is real, that he loves us and cares for us and is willing and able to be right there beside us in the most difficult of times. We truly are no longer the same when Jesus has touched us. Although the spiritual burden of guilt and shame cannot be seen in a physical sense, the result of that burden is often obvious by the bowed shoulders and frowning foreheads of those who experience it. It does not need to be like that. Jesus said "my yoke is easy and my burden is light". We do have a burden to carry in life, we have a specific purpose and job to do, but it is meant to be easy and light.

The Lord's Prayer

Those of us of the older generation will know the Lord's Prayer "off by heart", as even if we did not attend church, it was most probably used in school assemblies at least once a week. I don't know if Elvis ever sang this on stage, but it was recorded as part of an "informal session" of Elvis jamming with his friends and session musicians on 16th May 1971 in Studio B of the RCA recording studios in Nashville. Elvis would have known this prayer from his very early years as he regularly attended church with his parents and would often have recited it. It is called the Lord's Prayer because it is the prayer that the Lord Jesus taught his disciples to pray. Although I most often use a modern English translation of the Bible, Elvis would most probably know the Lord's Prayer in an older form of the English language. The following version which Elvis sings is from the American Standard Version:

Our Father which art in heaven
Hallowed be Thy name,
Thy kingdom come, Thy will be done,
On earth as it is in heaven.
Give us this day our daily bread and forgive us our debts
As we forgive our debtors
Lead us not into temptation
But deliver us from evil
For Thine is the kingdom and the power and the glory
For ever and ever
Amen.

Jesus taught this prayer to his disciples because they asked him to teach them how to pray. It must therefore be a perfect blueprint for effective prayer. This event is recorded in the Bible in Matthew chapter 6 and Luke chapter 11. The main elements of the prayer are recognition of God as our heavenly father, praising Him, proclaiming His authority, asking for physical needs and asking for forgiveness and for protection.

This version ends with proclamation of God's eternal rule. In different translations of the Bible, "debt" is translated as "trespasses", or "sins", but basically it is asking for forgiveness for anything we have thought, said or done, which is wrong. One important thing I learned when studying the Lord's Prayer, is that previously, I had not noticed that the forgiveness of God is conditional on us forgiving others. That can be very difficult and people sometimes say of others "I can never forgive them". Strong words – which we need to consider changing, if we really want to experience the lifting of that heavy burden of guilt and shame. I have seen many people find a release from pain and resentment, when they are able to say, "I forgive…"

Where No One Stands Alone
(Mosie Lister)

This song, recorded by Elvis in 1966 for the "How Great Thou Art" album, had been a hit for the Ink Spots in 1951. It's composer Mosie Lister was a member of the Statesmen Quartet, which also included Cat Freeman, Jake Hess, and Jim "Chief" Wetherington, with Hovie Lister on piano. Hovie recalls the following story of his encounter with Elvis and this song. It was after Elvis had come out of the army and The Statesmen were performing in Memphis, along with The Blackwood Brothers at one of the monthly Gospel Quartet Conventions. Elvis had come in the back door with his entourage of bodyguards and sat back stage. "One night", Hovie recalls, "he came in and we were on stage. I was sitting at the piano facing back stage and saw Elvis. Elvis said, "Where No One Stands Alone". We had about five minutes left of our time and I was trying to wrap up our program. Naturally I was getting ready for our finale, a fast song that would stir the crowd. And every time he would say "Where No One Stands Alone" and "How Long Has It Been". I could read his lips, but I would just shake him off, like a pitcher does a catcher. We did "Get Away Jordan" which was a fast song, one of those animated things where I jumped off the stage and everything. When I got through, everybody on stage was taking a bow and we were just tearing the place up. We were bent over bowing and couldn't see what was going on, just hearing the crowd applaud. I thought, 'My word we made a hit tonight!' All of a sudden I felt a hand on my shoulder. I turned round and it was Elvis. We hadn't known he was there on stage. He turned to me and said 'Tell Jake to leave the stage, we are going to do "How Long Has It Been" and "Where No One Stands Alone"'. So he sang those two songs and it absolutely tore up the audience. It was tremendous they were on their feet the whole time he sang both songs".

I guess this was one of Elvis' favourite songs, as it was what he sang as an impromptu performance at a concert in Montgomery, Alabama on February 16th 1977. A report of the show states, that this concert "showcased a unique highlight in his program. His still ever surfacing spontaneity caused him to perform a long forgotten tune. Suddenly he explained to the audience that he wanted to sing a gospel song that he had never performed on stage. While accompanying himself on the piano, he impressively performed *Where No One Stands Alone*, which ranks as one of the most outstanding and rarest performances of his career."

One can imagine Elvis' state of mind which prompted this performance. It was only six months before his death and he was really struggling, both physically and spiritually. We know that he felt so alone, perhaps feeling that the Lord was hiding his face from him, because of his not altogether godly lifestyle. When one is feeling so low, it is often difficult to remember that although it may appear that the Lord has deserted us, the truth is that He will never leave us nor forsake us. It is all too often our own sin that hides the Glory of God from us. Elvis did live like a king and indeed was called "the King". He had many worldly riches but was wise enough to know that that is not enough or even essential for happiness. In fact, he would know that riches can get in the way, as it did in the story Jesus told of the rich young ruler who did not enter the kingdom of heaven because he was unwilling to give up his worldly wealth. It was not the love of worldly riches, however, which troubled Elvis; he used them well, giving generously to others on many occasions. No it was the feeling of loneliness, so powerfully expressed in this song, which troubled him. It is a loneliness which is destructive and which nothing, apart from the knowledge of the everlasting love of a heavenly Father for us, can disperse.

I do believe that on August 16th 1977, Elvis was in fact taken to that place where no one stands alone, into the arms of his heavenly Father. I wonder how many of us know that although we may at times on earth experience great loneliness, that when we die, we know without doubt that we shall stand in that wonderful place where no one stands alone? That place which is guaranteed by our faith in the Lord and giver of life, Jesus Christ.

Chapter 4
Final Prayers

"Seek and you shall find" (Luke 11:9 - ASV)

Although I was not a fan at the time, I have heard and seen many recordings of Elvis in concert in the later seventies. He was still praising God, singing his heart out in "How Great Thou Art", but it was some of his secular songs as well as the gospel songs which were his desperate prayers to his heavenly Father. They were prayers of struggle, pain and regret, "(I'm so) Hurt", "You Gave Me A Mountain", "Help Me", "Separate Ways" and "Always On My Mind". Elvis first recorded this last song a few months before the separation from his wife, Priscilla, was formalised (the divorce was finalised in October 1973) and one can't help but feel that he is identifying with the words of the song; that he maybe hadn't always treated her 'quite as good as I should have' and that 'maybe I didn't take the time to tell her that 'I am so pleased that you are mine' or that he was 'so sorry I was blind and made you feel second best'.

I often wondered why the Bible is open at Psalm 40 in some frames of the video "He Touched Me, the Gospel Music of Elvis Presley". Admittedly it is difficult, but not impossible to read the artfully blurred image and identify it as Psalm 40. I asked Joe Moscheo, one of the Imperials who sang with Elvis and who was involved with the film, about this and he seemed to think that the Bible was randomly opened for the shot. If it was chosen deliberately then it is a good choice, if it was a random choice then it is amazing, because I would like to suggest that this psalm (prayer/song) of King David would exactly express Elvis' feelings in those last few months as he approached his death. As you read it for yourself, I believe you will see the parallels in Elvis' life.

To the chief Musician, A Psalm of David.
I waited patiently for the LORD; and he inclined unto me, and heard my cry.
He brought me up also out of an horrible pit, out of the miry clay, and set my feet upon a rock, and established my goings.
And he hath put a new song in my mouth, even praise unto our God: many shall see it, and fear, and shall trust in the LORD.
Blessed is that man that maketh the LORD his trust, and respecteth not the proud, nor such as turn aside to lies.
Many, O LORD my God, are thy wonderful works which thou hast done, and thy thoughts which are to us-ward: they cannot be reckoned up in order unto thee: if I would declare and speak of them, they are more than can be numbered.

Sacrifice and offering thou didst not desire; mine ears hast thou opened: burnt offering and sin offering hast thou not required.
Then said I, Lo, I come: in the volume of the book it is written of me,
I delight to do thy will, O my God: yea, thy law is within my heart.

I have preached righteousness in the great congregation: lo, I have not refrained my lips, O LORD, thou knowest.

I have not hid thy righteousness within my heart; I have declared thy faithfulness and thy salvation: I have not concealed thy loving-kindness and thy truth from the great congregation.

Withhold not thou thy tender mercies from me, O LORD: let thy lovingkindness and thy truth continually preserve me.

For innumerable evils have compassed me about: mine iniquities have taken hold upon me, so that I am not able to look up; they are more than the hairs of mine head: therefore my heart faileth me.

Be pleased, O LORD, to deliver me: O LORD, make haste to help me.

Let them be ashamed and confounded together that seek after my soul to destroy it; let them be driven backward and put to shame that wish me evil.

Let them be desolate for a reward of their shame that say unto me, Aha, aha.

Let all those that seek thee rejoice and be glad in thee: let such as love thy salvation say continually, The LORD be magnified.

But I am poor and needy; yet the Lord thinketh upon me: thou art my help and my deliverer; make no tarrying, O my God.   Psalm 40 (KJV)

A few hours before he died, Elvis prayed with his stepbrother, Rick Stanley: "Dear Lord please show me a way, I am tired and confused and I need your help". Elvis then said, "Rick we should all begin to live for Christ."

In the Bible passage where this theme, that "we should all begin to live for Christ" occurs (2 Corinthians 5:15), the main emphasis is on reconciliation. Jesus came to reconcile men to God, and those who want to live for Christ are urged to be ambassadors for God, to represent God on earth and have a ministry of reconciliation.

Elvis was an avid reader and certainly within the few weeks before he died, he was reading the "Scientific Search For The Face Of Jesus" and by some reports it was the book he was reading at the time of his death. This is a book which looks at the scientific evidence for Jesus, by examining the Turin shroud, which is a linen sheet that carries an imprinted image the front and the back of a crucified man, including the face. The imprint shows the peculiar characteristics that belong to a photographic negative. If Elvis was looking to science to support his faith in the crucified Christ, then he had slipped a long way from his original simple faith, but he was desperately searching for the spiritual Jesus, who himself exhorted us to ask in prayer "And I say unto you, 'Ask, and it shall be given you; seek and ye shall find, knock, and it shall be opened unto you. For every one that asketh receiveth; and he that seeketh findeth; and to him that knocketh it shall be opened.'"
Luke 11:9-10 (ASV)

I believe that all of Elvis' prayers were answered on the 16th August 1977.

Elvis' funeral was held in the music room at Graceland on Thursday August 18th. The service was planned by Vernon who asked a Memphis minister and friend of the family,

C. W. Bradley to preside. Reverend Rex Humbard preached a guest sermon and The Stamps Quartet, the Statesmen, Jake Hess, James Blackwood and Kathy Westmoreland did the singing. Songs included "The Lighthouse", "I Can Feel The Touch Of His Hand", "When It's My Time" all of which they knew were Elvis' favourites. Although the funeral was scheduled to last only half an hour, it went on for almost 2 hours. In his funeral sermon C.W. Bradley said:

"Words do not take away from a man's life and words do not add to a man's life in the sight of God. Though I will make several personal observations concerning Elvis, and from them seek to encourage us, it is not my purpose to try to eulogise him, this is being done by thousands throughout the world."

"We are here to honour the memory of a man loved by millions. Elvis can serve as an inspiring example of the great potential of one human being who has a strong desire and unfailing determination. From total obscurity Elvis rose to world fame. His name is a household word in every nook and corner of this earth. Though idolized by millions and forced to be protected from the crowds, Elvis never lost his desire to stay in close touch with humanity."

"In a society that has talked so much about the generation gap, the closeness of Elvis and his father and his constant dependence upon Vernon's counsel was heart-warming to observe. Elvis never forgot his family. In a thousand ways he showed his great love for them."

"In a world where so many pressures are brought upon us to lose our identity, to be lost in the masses, Elvis dared to be different. Elvis was different and no one can ever be exactly like him. Wherever and whenever his voice was heard, everybody knew that was Elvis Presley."

"But Elvis was a frail human being. And he would be the first to admit his weakness. Perhaps because of his rapid rise to fame and fortune he was thrown into temptations that some never experience. Elvis would not want anyone to think that he had no flaws or faults. But now that he is gone, I find it more helpful to remember his good qualities, and I hope you do too."

"We are here to offer comfort and encouragement to Elvis' family. There is much encouragement in all the beautiful flowers sent by loving hands and hearts from around the world. There is so much encouragement in the presence of so many who have crowded into our city in addition to those here. And also from knowing that literally millions throughout the earth have their hearts turned in this direction at this hour. There is also much encouragement from the beautiful music. But the greatest comfort and strength comes from knowing there is a God in heaven who looks upon us with love and compassion and who says, 'I will never leave you or forsake you!'"

Bradley then went on to quote from the hymn By S M T Henry "I Know My Heavenly Father Knows".

"We are here to be reminded that soon we too must depart this life. The Bible vividly emphasizes the brevity and uncertainty of life. Once when King Saul was chasing David across the country, David said "There is but a step between me and death" and none of us know when he shall take that step."

"Elvis died at 42. Some of you may not live to be that old. But it's not how long we live that is really important, but how we live. If we reject the Bible, then personally I find that life has no real meaning. The Bible teaches us that God's plans and purposes for man culminated in the death and resurrection of His son on a cross. Jesus lives today. And because He lives, through Him we too can have hope of a life beyond the grave.

Thus today I hold up Jesus Christ to all of us. And challenge each of you to commit your heart and life to Him. May these moments of quiet and thoughtful meditation and reflection of Elvis' life serve to help us to reflect upon our own lives and to re-examine our own lives. And may these moments help us to reset our compass. All of us sometime get going in the wrong direction".

Epilogue
Why?

In the year of the 25th anniversary of Elvis' death, this is a question which is increasingly being asked. It is a question which Elvis himself asked many times. Why did God give him such a wonderful voice and so much success? Why was he loved and admired by so many people? Others are now asking why is Elvis still so successful and one may say, even more popular today, with many more people becoming fans and being deeply moved by his music? Why is Elvis known worldwide? Someone once said that there are three names which are recognised all over the world. They are Jesus, Elvis and Coca Cola.

There were two comments I recently read in a well-known Elvis magazine, which I feel, reflect the thoughts of many people. One was from Bill Burk, the editor of the magazine and a friend of Elvis. "How deeply Elvis touched so many millions of lives during his lifetime; and continues to do so has never ceased to amaze me. And it crosses political, financial and social boundaries". The other is in the form of a question, from Kathy Braquet a fan from Texas who wrote: "What is it about this one man that keeps thousands of fans coming back (to Memphis) year after year from all over the world...... It's obviously his God given talent/voice, his sensuous gorgeous looks, his deep spirituality and his kindness to others. But it goes *much* further than all of that. It's something that blows my mind and I can't seem to put my finger on."

Since I became an Elvis fan in 1995, I have also been amazed and continue to be so by the phenomenon that Elvis is. After researching into his life, particularly the influence of the gospel in his life, I have discovered many things and have come to the following conclusion, which you may like to consider.

Elvis' upbringing in the "Bible Belt" in the 1930s and '40s, where attending church two or three times a week was normal, ensured that he had a great love for God, a good knowledge of the Scriptures and that he knew how to pray. When they moved to Memphis, his parents made sure that they had a good church to belong to, and having met their pastor Rev Rex Dyson, I am convinced that his passionate preaching had a great effect on the young teenage Elvis. When they moved to the Assemblies of God Church, Elvis would continue to get good teaching, but was perhaps not so involved. After Elvis started travelling and became famous, he no longer had time to attend church regularly, and in any case was concerned that his presence caused a stir and took the focus off God. He got his preaching from the television evangelists, and his praise took the form of many hours of singing gospel songs, before, after and in between the shows, with his backing singers such as The Imperials and JD Sumner and the Stamps. At one stage in the '70s he even had his own gospel group, "Voice", whom he employed to sing gospel whenever he required, which often was late at night and into the early hours of the morning.

It is clear that Elvis had many godly characteristics: beauty, kindness, a sweet nature, a sense of humour, generosity and an interest in and a desire to help people. His lifestyle, however, did not always reflect the holiness of the awesome God whom he served. There were many forces in his life attempting to lead him away from God, and I am amazed that he kept his sweet nature till the end, even in the face of the most vicious attacks. It certainly is a case of "amazing grace".

Having been brought up as a Christian, Elvis knew that he was on earth not only to live a good life and to help people but also that the Lord had a specific purpose for his life. He endeavoured throughout his life to discover that purpose.

It was his desire to be a full time gospel singer. At the time of his death he had already discussed in detail and planned a full gospel concert. I believe also that he was called to be an evangelist, that is, not only to sing of God's goodness and love and to give hope, but also, to bring people to a point of recognition of the need of redemption which comes only through Jesus Christ.

So, if this was God's plan for Elvis' life, what went wrong? I would maintain that nothing went wrong, in the sense that God's purposes for Elvis' life are still being worked out. It is true, that if Elvis had made a strong and determined effort to break free, he could still be alive travelling the world, singing, preaching and leading many people into the Kingdom of God. As it was, Elvis was caught in a trap. I believe the Lord knew that Elvis would not be able to get out of this trap, so in His mercy he took him from this scene of time and I believe Elvis now sees Jesus face to face and is having a ball singing gospel forever, as the song says "we've no less days to sing God's praise than when we first began."

Perhaps Elvis is a type of Samson. Samson was an anointed man of God, who served God well, by destroying God's enemies with his exceptional strength, but because of his moral weakness, he lost his strength, was captured and was reduced to being mocked in front of his enemies. Through his death, however he destroyed more of God's enemies (did more for God) than when he was alive. *(Samson's story can be found in the Bible in the book of Judges 13 –16.)*

Perhaps it will be that through his tragic death, which has captured the imaginations of millions and helped to continue the "mystery" of Elvis, Elvis will have reached more people with the gospel than when he was alive. There are many stories of people who came to accept the gospel of Jesus Christ when Elvis was alive, as a result of attending a concert, or listening to recordings of him singing the gospel songs. Since Elvis' death, more people have become Christians, listening to the gospel songs or even while standing by the graveside at Graceland.

So that is why I have come to the conclusion that what it is about this man, is the Holy Spirit. Elvis' lifestyle was not exemplary in holiness, but Elvis was given a gift to communicate the Gospel and the gifts of God cannot be revoked, therefore the charisma of that gift was very attractive whether or not he used it fully. People are still attracted to and hungry for the anointing of the Holy Spirit, and the presence of love, which was so evident in his life.

Why Elvis was and is still so famous and loved is I believe, because God's plan for Elvis' life was that hundreds of thousands of people would hear the gospel through him and be saved. Although Elvis is dead, God is not, and by His Holy Spirit, still reaches out to us to let us know that He loves us passionately and does not desire for any of us to perish.

Most fans are horrified by the people who "worship" Elvis in an open physical way. These "worshippers" bow down and kneel before statues of him and look to him to answer their prayers. Elvis consumes almost every aspect of their lives. Most people inherently know that this is wrong and yet one wonders how many "ordinary" fans do in fact worship Elvis without really realising it. I was recently speaking to an "ordinary" Elvis fan who is very happily married and living a very normal life. When I asked, "How would you feel if for some reason you would never be able to listen to Elvis singing again; for example if you went deaf, or all of Elvis' recordings disappeared from the face of the earth?" His reply was, "It would be the end of the world. There would be no more reason to live without Elvis. Elvis is everything to me."

Could it be that many fans in their attitude to Elvis are worshipping, not Elvis, but an "unknown God". They see in Elvis something desirable, but cannot quite define what it is. Perhaps it is similar to the situation that the Athenians were in when the apostle Paul found their altar inscribed "TO AN UNKNOWN GOD". Paul said to them, "Now what you worship as something unknown I am going to proclaim to you. The God who made the world and everything in it is the Lord of heaven and earth and does not live in temples built by hands. And he is not served by human hands, as if he needed anything, because he himself gives all men life and breath and everything else. From one man he made every nation of men, that they should inhabit the whole earth; and he determined the times set for them and the exact places where they should live. God did this so that men would seek him and perhaps reach out for him and find him, though he is not far from each one of us. 'For in him we live and move and have our being.' As some of your own poets have said, 'We are his offspring.' Therefore since we are God's offspring, we should not think that the divine being is like gold or silver or stone—an image made by man's design and skill. In the past God overlooked such ignorance, but now he commands all people everywhere to repent. For he has set a day when he will judge the world with justice by the man he has appointed (Jesus). He has given proof of this to all men by raising him from the dead." *(Acts 27:23-31)*

These words are as true and relevant today as they were when they were first written.

So next time you listen to Elvis singing gospel remember that he was a servant of God bringing a message of hope to you. And it does indeed "go further than that". God is still alive, only a prayer away, waiting for our response to his ultimate gift. For He so loved everyone in the world, that He gave his only son Jesus that all who believe in him may not perish but have eternal life. It is, as Kathy says, "something that blows our minds" and may perhaps elicit that "trembling" question, "what must I do to be saved?"

Perhaps if he were still alive, Elvis would say something like this to us:
"You can just say about all that Gospel stuff **Return To Sender** because **I've Got A Lot of Livin'** to do. You can also say that religion is just a kind of **Good Luck Charm** - only a bit of superstition to make you feel better when you get **All Shook Up** once in a while, or regret paying the heavy price for **One Night Of Sin**. Some however are afraid that they're too bad and that it is too late for **A Fool Such As I** and that they have missed their chance of finding God. Some fear they've **Lost That Lovin' Feeling** for the things of God they once had, and that's that. But **I Believe** that God gives us another chance. You may feel deep down about God, that **You're Always On My Mind** and when the chips are down and I'm left to my thoughts, **I Just Can't Help Believin'**, but beware, **It's Funny How Time Slips Away...** I tell you **Doncha Think it's Time?** to **Reconsider Baby.**

Are You Lonesome Tonight? Is there an emptiness in your heart? If you feel stirred and moved and would really like to know the Lord for real, perhaps for you **It's Now Or Never.** When you think of Jesus dying on the cross you may not understand all about it, but **If That Isn't Love**, nothing is. Many before you have said **Where Could I Go But To The Lord?** It is easy to begin that relationship with Jesus, even a simple prayer sincerely said is how you can **Put Your Hand In The Hand (Of the Man From Galilee)**. All I can say is

that when anyone is willing to **Reach Out To Jesus** they will know in their heart **He Touched Me**, and then they will want to sing for all to hear **How Great Thou Art.**

Only Believe and there will be everlasting **Life** and **Peace In The Valley** for you."